Hyphasis

T0164285

Lyndon Davies was born and brought up in Cardiff. He studied English at Aberystwyth University, since when he has lived in various parts of England, France and Wales, supporting himself with jobs varying from gravedigger to campsite courier to physiotherapy assistant. He is currently living in Powys with his wife – a painter – combining freelance writing with doing up an old house.

Hyphasis

Lyndon Davies

Parthian
The Old Surgery
Napier Street
Cardigan
SA43 1ED

www.parthianbooks.co.uk

First published in 2007
© Lyndon Davies 2007
All Rights Reserved

ISBN 1-905762-11-9
    978 1905762 11 8

Cover design by Marc Jennings
Inner design by books@lloydrobson.com
Printed and bound by Dinefwr Press, Llandybïe, Wales

Published with the financial support of the Welsh
Books Council

British Library Cataloguing in Publication Data
A cataloguing record for this book is available from the
British Library

This book is sold subject to the condition that it shall
not by way of trade or otherwise be circulated without
the publisher's prior consent in any form of binding
or cover other than that in which it is published and
without a similar condition including the condition
being imposed on the subsequent purchaser

Contents

Effigies

For Pen

The Sacrifice

No improvement ever,
and the vista woolly,
and the ghosts indifferent.

Finally I sold the saxophone.

Quitting the Premises

One at a time they enter, at maddeningly
regular intervals. You could check your calendar,
your watch...
Here's the drill: a scuffle at the threshold,
followed by footsteps, slurred but becoming clearer,
neater;
each sick howl modulating to a hum
of baffled insolence, which is when you'd get them
and break them: the clods, the callow ones, just to see
the juice slew out –
at the merest touch, at the merest whisper.

It becomes frustrating,
there's nothing to get your teeth into,
or that gets its teeth into you, though the time
is ripe (desolation honed on its echo),
deserves its brawl, its rebuttal. What gathers,
ravening, beyond the pieties of the public square,
is yours to long for, is yours to call to,
stamping that hoof...

When you least expect it
air shunts in the corridor, somebody breathing hard
goes rattling past in a pother, shaking a sword
and yodelling; is gone before you've even managed
to point the lens or prepare the seismograph –
to lessen it by any scale of reckoning,
this Great Event, this phenomenon, which you,
admit it, could never have hoped for nor imagined,
but have to go on imagining forever.

Better to leave, though, while you know you can,
by following a thread which ends at your feet,
down many corridors, none of them distinctive
except the last – that's the one where daylight
blares from the opening and a crowd heaves through
to greet you; although, when they see you coming,
the silence drops like a shutter; the throng
gives way before you, cleaves like a rotten fruit;
for you are not the one they were expecting.

Amores

1.
My vigilance did not disturb her,
but the tethers had to go,

and the dirty photographs in the album.
Bristling through like a sirocco,

she scoured my body raw.
Still, when my body thinks of her

it is not with bitterness, but with desire
for the wound she made me bear.

2.

Frost on the grass,
moonlight over the frost:
there's nothing here that will yield
to anything we ask,
or ask anything of us.

The garden has hardened
into itself. Every shrub's
a blot on the shimmer
of irradiative metals.
Lawn, woodpile, cedar,
all's still and resolved,
but for us –

just to look
is to seal forever
the knowledge that undoes,
that rips
what the frost knits.

3.

One night the moon
burst open like a fig.

One night the honey-flood
raved through the garden.

I saw her neck bend under it
like a green twig.

4.

Halfway up a cedar of Lebanon
the discussion centering on the fold
apparent in every manifestation
of sexual and political oppression
finally calmed down. It was peaceful sitting there,
but cold,
high up in the cedar of Lebanon.

The Collier Elsewhere

The Watchers

None of the crows are shocked
by his reduced appearance.

They settle their feathers
and patrol the roof-tree.

The Coming

All I have to do is stand here
at the threshold of the adit,
for the rain filleting down
at an unlikely angle
to work its magic. Soon
there's a pool of ink at my feet,
tarn-black.
This seeps away
quite gradually into the landscape's
hidden soughs and corridors.
Eventually,
someone leaning out
over the little brook in the village
far away down there, might catch
a glimpse of shadow, a stain
flashing past in the torrent, and look up
at the hill and see me
waving one empty hand, nude, pink
as a sugar mouse.

Rite

The shift begins
with a plummeting sensation.

Look – we are falling,
things are falling,

out of the dark
and into the frame of light.

If ever we arrive
everything will arrive with us:

soup, hearts, chronicles –
a raw heap
of wobbling mucus...

But we could be flying,

we could be flying,
innocent as the stone
which shattered the window
of the dream-racked chapel.

The Titans

They are not yet bound,
their fires squirm all night,
all day, like whips,
like banners. The wind's spiked
with their rage. Their shouts
are hammerblows.
We crouch
in the stall, half-choked,
but messages keep arriving
from further out –
the abnormal places,
where our lost ones scrabble.
Sometimes it's cosy though,
tucked away in this fold
where facets wink
from the face and we
wink back. It's a shock
to come up in daylight:
sun's gimlet
pierces your eye,
and space opens up
like a terrible amphitheatre
patrolled by jets,
by basilisks, by crows.

Saving the Furniture

You cannot sit easy
at table, or sleep
like a baby, knowing
in your heart that the chair
you slumped in, the bed
you wallowed in, defeated,
is no longer your own;

that the table groaning
into its metamorphosis, under a pang
of fork-ends, that jade,
may yet buck and throw
its bread-sops on the floor,
its tea-slops on the ceiling.

What were we to do
but go out that night,
disturbing the dew?
A baluster in moonlight
has its own virtue;
a splat with the spray
of stars on it is a strand
on some dark lagoon
in some unimaginable land.

All along the backs, though,
they were leaping the fences:
glass winked, a sideboard
soared like a thoroughbred.
You would have believed
they flew, that their lives

depended on it,
but it wasn't *their* lives.

We wondered if we would ever
see them again
in the old way, or want to
if ever they came back
still hurdling the moon,
like spirits; the cat
running in with the spoon.

Beyond

We heard it shift in the rock; we heard it
groan in the timberwork. All along the levels
niggling and growling. Praise be, the props
were sound
(sufficiently elegant, in their own fashion –
curving neatly off, receding
beyond the holocausts). We wondered
what would happen if our lamps went out,
but there is always light and the roof
stays up.

There is something moving yet
in the rock, above us, under us, some mad worm
unravelling its coils. We will never be safe
until that worm sleeps.

The Crossing

From there, through Samarra,
with occasional rest-stops,
I followed that map
until I came to the desert
of all deserts, where nothing else
stood in my way,
just a curious rabbit
and a straggle of Joshua trees
gesticulating blankly.

My boots crunched
over clay-shards bristling
with script of a kind
entirely unknown to me,
which I found I could read
without making sense of:
it passed through my skin,
through my blood,
and my limbs led the way

to scattered encampments
where people shared water
freely. We talked
and they gave me directions
such as this: "Hang a left
at the Devil's Golf Course,
carry straight on
to Mosaic Canyon,
keeping the sun
above you at all times,
the moon in your calabash,
and your camera handy."

I have to admit
I could not take them seriously
and went my own way.
Then the wind got frisky
and sand filled my eyes –
I was starting to struggle.
But luckily two serpents
took me in hand.

Then we made steady progress
to the fabled city,
city of all cities,
which is where you find me.
Along buckled terraces
attenuated figures
peeped from the brick-piles.
Not a house was standing.

When we came to a temple,
we stretched out in its shade,
took water and a little
dried meat. I was happy
to rest there a while,
but the air grew heavy,
ominous, with the sour musks
of decay.

Then I longed
for the desert again.
I was up and going, too,
when they showed me that brick
in a wall of the temple:

one narrow brick, low,
near the base – I crouched
to examine it. Though the script
was barely legible,
pestled away
by millennia, there was no
mistaking that name
engraved on the brick
in the wall of the temple,
in the city of all cities,
in the desert of all deserts.
It was my own name.

And I sat down and wept.
I sat down and I wept.

Tonypandy

Stones share our luck,
unfold our grievances
in a shop's lap;
elevate our passions,
crack! in the poked eye
of a chapel. Every wit
his fling, his rare sling
of considering fibres.

A stone delights
in the palm. Boulders though
are difficult, require
persuasion
and a steep hill,
then go their own way,
shock-headed, although they too
arrive when they must.

A celestial tucket
gives them all wings:
their work done,
they flutter straight to their place,
straight up at last to their place
on the sphere. Then the edifice
is complete again.

But the bullet stays here,
the bullet stays here
in its wound forever,
anonymous from the start,
indifferent from the outset,

like a mathematician
solving equations.

Fragment

"Illusion," it said, "is the gift; the truer
part of you;
is in the nature of a gap,
still smoking, between the shock-wave and the blast.
Though personal, strictly personal, it contains
so much a vision couldn't do without:
low hills receding towards violet, clouds
like beaten egg-whites:
picture it!
When you think
of what was missing, though...

"When I think
of everything that was missing, ash
flutters down from my hand,
the other bleeds rust,
flakes rust,
(it's certain that there are fires
beyond our will or capacity). A shadow
is over the tent.
To begin to tell you
of what we lost, what we held, and why,
between the coloured rocks and the pyramid-
shaped slag-heaps,
knowing that you would suffer as much
to hear it as we had suffered, as I
must suffer the gap that spares me,
the gap that tears me...

"I move my hand –
its colours leeching into that pure stream
which troubles your sleep at last. It's the shock,

the smack of it:
incendiary molecules."

In Little

No longer viable,
laughed at intimately,
we performed wonders
of scornful diligence,

grew adept,
disappeared almost completely
in the minutiae
where dread swallows itself.

Sermon

You were expecting me at this point
to speak, no?
To say my piece; to exert
my eloquence upon some matter ripe
for the treatment:
the price of thorns;
the city that rose like a loaf,
then flubbered down in a hoo-hah of trumpets and gongs...

But there are so many ferns to part
on the tump,
so many steps to the rostrum,
that by the time I get there
I have forgotten everything I had to say
when I set out;
and all that rises to my tongue's
a slick,
a slurry of stone-muck,
blood, bile, tar,
seething up to swamp me:
a complete vocabulary
rotting into the flux like old stumps in a bog,
old trunks.

Hyphasis*

* At the Hyphasis river the men, exhausted, homesick, rain-soaked, refused to follow Alexander any further. When it became clear that he could not persuade them, he shut himself away in his tent for three days.

No Man's Land

Whoever lingers now
in the mudfields,
rots,

whoever falters,
whoever
grieves now
for the covenant.

Sheaved
sarissas mouldering.

And in our blankets
serpents
and in our clothes...

Maenads

That was the worst thing I found out:
the voices clamouring beyond the walls,
so many, extending to kingdom come,

will shatter your peace at last, they'll scatter you
all over;
they'll kibble your bones to a powder.

Once: the distinguished landing, volitions
walloping open like sky-rockets,
like like like.... And so it went on.

Oracle

In cisterns, in buckets,
demijohns, milk-bottles,
test-tubes, cups of tea,
in buttes, in beer-glasses,
tear-ducts, saliva-
pools, blood-bags; the glistening
mercury of barometers;
what rock hid away,
earth jammed to its marrow,
quivers in a ripple,
becoming visible
to the eye, the ear;
or in a thumb's maze,
swirled grain of a table's
written
and erased.

Each sealed detonation,
each sanguinary bellow
of love or power,
storming the aquifers.

Orphic

Rot set in
with the first twang
of the mystical air.

Sepsis began
softening the strings,
smouldering in a gate.

Nobody saw him
pass, go down
into that clean field.

Despair
devoured everything,
including the catafalque.

The Death of Cleitus

He fell with his arms thrown open.
Yes, he was trying to save my life
when I killed him.

In his avowed opinion
a life ought to go on being recognisable.

Then the shields would tally and hold true
forever:

I call it The Eternal Rescue
(irksome to all parties concerned).

Anthropology

I passed through a place
where it seldom rains:
the people are clothed
in dust, in fine dust
of radiant colours,
but the glare's so harsh
over the dunes and the salt-flats,
the eye cringes back –

they are all but invisible
to each other. If they want
to see what they're missing
they must rise at dawn,
or stay awake at sunset,
when rays sweep low
over chemical ramparts.
But nobody bothers with that.

They navigate by sighs,
make love at random,
finger the crow's prints, the snake's fosse,
through adobe canyons.

Crucible

When I consider Macedonia
I remember Anselm Kiefer's lead books,
which require a strong arm and a strong floor;
an ability to resist poison.

The lyrical blankness of his skies,
it could be; or that insidious flakiness
of the light:
old sediments, dead effects.
I turn the pages over until the last

shy revenant, weighing less than nothing,
replaces all the books on the shelves
over the enervated floorboards.
Macedonia closes the equation at this point.

Home

A settled map, the necessity
for carrying on repeating yourself;

for following the same paths under limes
lit up by coloured bulbs at Christmas,

or in summer drifting a clean tang
over the edge of the common acres

where the street gathers you and you hear
an absence muttering from every hedge.

Merus

This all happened before the rain began:
now it's a sunny bank-holiday, and here
they come, the people, crying "Ite Bacchai!",
across a ridge, disorderly, in high spirits,

pissed. Where the laurel glints and the ivy
nods on the pergola: it is the place,
they know it, it is the place. All the springs
are gushing out like anthems, the paths are bathed.

And here they come, crying "Ite Bacchai!"
cleaving the light,
ravishing the light.

Keynotes

History's vatic rap
quietens now in this gap, this minimum
which we go on witholding and witholding,
beyond violence
and beyond expenditure;

who would have suffered the same cost
again,
given that advice, given those
impediments.

But was the lost word spoken?
And is the task in hand?

Chant

Death is empty
death is clean

is empty
is clean

death
is death is

empty
is clean

death is
death is

The Fun-Pavilion

Other people have different lives:
they want to renovate the Fun-Pavilion
and will do too, given half a chance.

There will be summer music, tap-dancers, comedians
by the score:
a succession of enticing acts
which fizzle out eventually and are forgotten
eventually,
when the hoardings are brought down.

Effigies

The Space of Saying

Maurice Blanchot

We are not talking here about the blind men
staggering across a landscape entirely
foreign to them: one falls then the others
fall,
but where were they going? Where
were they going anyway –

the beggars, the tramps, the scarecrows?
We are not talking about a dance,
not yet,
it's just an orderly procession
of well-appointed citizens; except, for now,
the leader must follow the others down the path,

and move when they move, hurry when push
comes to shove,
and try to go on when the panic
takes him; and never, never ever to turn his head
to the one who tracks him, the imminence that grips his ribs
in the half-light:
the one they are effortlessly gaining upon.

Pilgrim

Geoffrey Chaucer

I was there, I travelled with them
into the flatlands, keeping to the path
for fear of marshes.
Some of them ran ahead
and some ran off at a tangent. It was my job
to call the fool a fool and the wise man lucky

for travelling further than the ground they'd stood on.
At night you could hear the chants, see incense
curdling amongst the rafters of an inn;
that oriel blush on the hams. When they broached their stories
some of them were told by their stories.
Well, I avoided them.

We found we were getting nowhere, were going
nowhere.
The place was cavernous and ill-lit.
Words swarmed in the niches, straw poked, an occasional spark
flew out from its housing. It was my job
to laugh at the funny bits and to lose the horses.

The Banner

Akira Kurosawa

Of the several colours, the myriad tints,
of the hints, the nuances of a myriad avatars
of that one colour – shade, tone, voice –
occurring naturally or otherwise
(sky-notes,
earth, water-notes, fire-glints), it's up to you
to choose the ones already chosen for you –
to take them to heart and run with them; to choose
the forms too,
configurations of belligerent metal,
already chosen, for you of all people
fortunate or otherwise: the flag unfurled
in the war-place, path to the citadel, tomb,
relations, counsellors; and be ready at once to hurl
wherever those clours waver, wherever
those colours fade and the different colours
fume in the leaves,
that incredible crimson shout.

Text

Marguerite Duras

More or less always,
more or less anywhere –
the guilt that dazzles you.
Treason in the sheets;
fear in the blind-slats.

This body lies down
in heat. There are many
things you can do
to a body. You might
interrogate it "roughly".

A flower grows through it
suddenly and is picked
and thrown away:
sweet melancholy bloom,
without name or provenance.
All name, all provenance.

Watch

T S Eliot

The eye of the flame grows weak,
more distant ever,
as Truth closes in.

All over the campsite, logs
like shimmering honeycombs
collapse into cinders;

night moulds its tableaux:
sanctums, chambers of mourning.

History is a face
the coyote tears at,
somewhere out there in the cold.

It is time to prepare our beds.

The Just

Henry Fonda

You were normal and it hurt us
to see the way they treated you,
because we knew they would treat us the same:
our heads would spout, ring out, in chiaroscuro
ditches;
the bars would clang on our shame.

You kept your head up, though your shoulders sagged
perceptibly under the weight of the coming
outrage. You were ordinary, god help you,
but marked:
you couldn't quite fit your limbs
to the shadow under the buzzard's wings.

You had to go through it all from the start,
and come out ready to begin.
That was your genius, though – to learn something
and bring it home to dinner in the evening:
meat-loaf and homilies with the wife and kids.

Emanations

Anselm Kiefer

1.

Because it's broken now and because
it's scattered,
the spirit wakes, takes part
in the transformations.
At the foot of a ladder,
at the foot of a railway-track,
on the boring beach,
it summons the serpent that will make it whole.
The serpent –
a wire that speaks; a funnel
that concentrates every cloud; a coil
in the seed; a governance in the wheat:
such spaces blaze in the body of a serpent,
swelling and thinning, rising and falling.
It could be here that the spirit will take flight
on its wings of lead,
on its skis of iron,
over the straw-flecked granary
to that gold-flecked vision.

2.

You turned away from the forest,
which baffled you but whose beasts were real.
You were never the one with the adze, but the room
admits you anyway: its neat rows
of assimilated pine-logs,
its nude planks,
help you to pause, consider the giants
and the dybbuks.
It may be you will light a flame
of rushes dipped in resin from still-drooling boards:
twelve flames at equal intervals. You can stay,
or come again when you need to
or never come again.

There is nothing sacred about it, there are only
the flames,
which are not sacred. The flames recall
to the ordered woodpile, assimilated forest,
what was belied, begotten there: a kind
of anguish, a kind
of goety in the grain.

3.

The book gets heavier with every passing moment.
Soon you'll require a pulley, or a fork-lift truck
just to get it down off the shelf.
And what then?
And how will you ever get the covers open?

It makes you long for those wide open spaces.
If only you could make a start, though, arrive
at page one, say,
but the page is fading
even as you look at it – bits crumble off.
The whole thing is falling apart and you with it.

Your arms grow weak, your capacity to engage
deserts you: you're just a quavering in the air...
But all is not lost, there's somebody else there:
he greets you;
he knew you were coming. He says
that he is the Jew in the book and the book is the Jew (Jabès).

Arc

John Donne

Never mind the nuisance
of alleged departures –
the compass swings, splits
to define an amplitude.
Man is a compass.

Man is a string
stretched tight, from the choiry
dome to the abattoir.
But who plucks the note?
(Be true to me, love,
until our flesh drops
like a clutch of underthings.)

We can only kiss
because we have braved
those ravages of the pulpit
raised on our differences.

Tincture

S T Coleridge

Dumbstruck, I struggled out from that mêlée,
clutching the rose. In spite of everything –
blight, apathy, contusions – there it was in my fist
(locked tight for punching, probably; or for playing
that game – what is it?
Something to do with potatoes).

I stumbled into the living-room, clutching the bloom
that sealed my journey, was about to second it
in the eyes of the other. O my god, that upright
legible, reliable citizen – there he was, looking on,
with his sour wit and his haemorrhoids.

He could have taken it from me as a gift,
from the mulch below the monolith – that most decorous
stern watchtower.
It might have been of use
as a kind of landscape, say: a panorama
fit for rambling over,
fit for remarking upon.

Looking On

Emily Dickinson

I, on the other hand,
did not need a ticket
or an invitation.
I slipped round the back:
the classic attack.

I love the stones,
they are funny, they want
to say one thing,
just one thing
and go home.

It's a dangerous matter
to uncover your ears
when a sky weeps,
when a mountain blows its nose.
Keep low.

Domestic

Igor Stravinsky

Putting my hat aside for a moment,
putting aside my cane, my carte-de-séjour,
my buttonhole; putting aside my ring
engraved with the crest of the harlequin,
my politesse,
my deeply ingrained sense of duty, fair-play, hospitality;

I swung the axe and the guest went down
like a sack of logs. I swung it, the axe bit
and the guest went down and stayed down: the illustrious
guest,
the one with his finger on the pulse,
his fist on the pulse.

After that I forgot I was ever going out,
and started in on the furniture. It was possible to construct
from what was left, and even as the pieces flew,
a guest more pliable, less "true",
who'd rig a deck (if he had to),
but who never declared war on anyone.

Brimham Rocks

William Shakespeare

Rocks by wind-lathe
chiselled, gouged, grooved:
bed-knob, basilica,
plate-stack, minaret, womb;
where fog grips, blackens
and a birch drips.
That way I took,
by tower, by battlement, by ditch,
is hard to the hand,
grates muscle. Through cleft,
through ginnel, tracking
that lost name.
Through fog
into fog, shape muttering
to shape: prophetic
light-guzzling crones.

The Damage

Georg Baselitz

It's no to everything except the damage
ripening in each infested cellar,
each tumulus, each padlocked room; forever
no to the light which soothes, which laves;
the grammar, the flutes, the elegies, the constellations.

Now I know and I know I know
why the eagle tumbled. I spit hard, gob
on the minerals and work them in and they do my bidding.
Bleak? It's so bleak the angels shriek
in the spectra, clamping their fat eyes shut.

And I grind them in with the rest of it, and mud shrieks
with pollen of angels. Pay no attention to this
(the quarry gibbering in the mouth of the eagle):
my head's on wrong, all the colours are upside down.
The flux runs into the soil with a gorgeous yammer.

Imperium

Henry Purcell

We are talking tragedy here, a degree of upset
liable to burn a hole in the fire-back:
he, with a blush, is following his star,
but she's had enough of all that malarkey
and sits down quietly with her servant and begins to fade.

It's no good moaning about it: every day
begins with a cliché, ends with a commonplace.
But everything in between is the kingdom –
what happens there is for real and for money:
definitive, death-bound, vital.

When he turns away
denial runs through the core of her like a blade –
remove it, the sap commences flowing,
tissues degrade, there is a general withering
of the light.
But space is available and space
is weird, is weird.

Radioactive

Antonin Artaud

For the final ritual of the evening
everyone held hands and danced in a ring
around the spoiltip, stamping their feet
and shimmying as if their lives depended on it;
closing the circle gradually, moving in
on that rubble-cone, lit up like the pomegranate trees
of Dis,
with erotic fruit, malign fruit,
and crunching it down to atoms beneath their boots,
their fists.

No wonder the creature stirs
on the top, and lifting his head from his armpit,
licks his lips and ullulates like an old-
fashioned red-indian. His territory is diminishing
fast: it's a toss-up whether the poison
mounting their limbs will rise quickly enough
to assist.
Already some of them are on their knees
calling for unction as their lights go pop;

some others are ripping their togs off – it seems to them
they are fading away. It's hideous: the male
and the female sexual organs have got mixed up
in the ruck – each fused with its opposite. He gobbles them
down for dinner, suddenly going off
like a missile, a glowing stone in his mouth;
is hurtling away to everywhere at once.

Listening In

Ludwig van Beethoven

This is what it takes:
it takes everything,
though little gets through.
A tree's heart shivers
in the gloom of a forest.

The world's heart shivers
in the tree's heart.

Druid's Altar

i.m. Dai Davies 1918-1999

You can wait all day for the heron,
it's going to shock you anyway – clattering out
from the very alder-clump you most suspected
of harbouring what, at that time, in no way
resembled anything that could terrorize the leaves,
or tear that yelp from your chest.
It's necessary
to concentrate all day on the one thing,
but fail at it;
for your greed to falter,
if only for an instant: say, when the cat jumps up
for the fly, or the phone goes, or that opalescent lustre
under the great magnolia-tree seems suddenly grey,
unappetising even, bringing to mind the dead
who wait all day in their beds, not waiting
for anything really – the heron has already burst
from their tree;
they have learned to live with it, as you must now.

Le Maudit Maudit

Arthur Rimbaud

Even I – it's hysterical – have to keep coming back
to the campfire. There is no corner of the dark
unmollified by its gems, unedified by its wink:
the shrine in the garden, shire where a kettle hissed
to the gas-light
and mother muttered to father.

Even I, who'd forgotten ever having propped my jaw
in a hen's bordello, or listened in a barn
to rain on the roof; the power-hum in the core
of grain-sack and wood-stack; couldn't resist forever
the plush of it –
sweet gravity of the intimate spaces.

Poetry, though, has no comforts: that demonic
pageant created turbulence in a high chamber;
its degradations flickered all night on the mairie,
and grocers stumbled over their knobbed canes
when sonnets went off like gunshots.

White-Out

Cora Sandel

Everything I needed to say about the snow
eludes me now: every clause, each adjective,
frost-ravaged, chafed to the bone, is white
on white. But snow keeps coming and the bones
are buried deep as the celandine, as the lark's flight.

I couldn't see what I needed to see
on waking. A lustre broods on the gloom;
its thin devotional glimmer pervades the room
and consecrates the ceiling. This is a light
which strands:
the shame of the wardrobe turns from the shame of the tallboy.

Snow blocks the doors and divides the villages:
each separate wish in its separate reliquary.
I lie in wait for the dawn, for the smell of coffee
to open a cloaca, to spill its guts.
The rosary of the breath counts out its beads.

Country Boy

Robert Frost

It is pleasant to converse:
a bit like manoeuvering an old cart
over the ruts and bosses of a track,
and pausing from time to time and listening
to all the sounds of the wood;

or crossing a bridge, or a crossing,
and drifting-off a piece, sure that the beast
will go on lumbering homeward the way it knows
as well as the sound of its own hoofs
cuffing the stones.

Except for all that Greek stuff, that river thing...
Anyway, I like my neighbour (why shouldn't I?):
the way we meet and diverge
within the exchange of terms. That happy chance:
our looking over the wall at the exact same moment!

From the Battlements

Rainer Maria Rilke

Knowing that there is silence,
especially here where the storm
blowing from no direction
rants in the turret-tops;

and that all is open now
through a lancet window, slim
as an asparagus-stick, begrimed
by the siege you shut your eyes on,
by soot, by cordite;

and that when you lie asleep
pure waters descending
from distant glaciers
ripple through your mouth's
raw pit, like a spirit
fluttering in a charnel-house;

you begin to speak
and everything you abandoned,
waiting, who'd thought
you could never wait long enough
with sufficient reason,
gathers in the courtyard.

Next Door

Samuel Beckett

Mother and father
have only popped out
for a moment. Why then
are the cupboards howling?
Why is the stove cold
as a stela, the ghoulie
snivelling in its cistern?

They thought we were tucked up,
away with the fairies.
One thing is sure:
when mother and father
come back, reparations
will sweeten the house,
if the house stands.

Founding

Lewis Mumford

Bearing in mind that ditch
which girdled the city like a ring of scurf
thrown up by a flood, some wilderness-haunting tide
of the fables,
though those of us on the outside
know better than that, better than anyone,

what toxins seep from the walls, what rot
from the body politic; from avenues paved with law
what effluent, what slop;
dead cats, dead gladiators;
bearing in mind all that,
we turn our face from the wind and begin again

putting brick on brick and stone on stone.
Each gem-bright edifice will quickly dim,
but that doesn't stop us. The important thing
is getting the drains laid.

Somebody may come
who knows how to live there, finally.
I say "may".

Climbing the Wall

Giuseppe Verdi

In the end it's the usual horror-movie,
minus the monster;
or the room's the monster:
the room devours him, shackled him from the start,
attrition darkening the sheets and the silverware.
Now walls close in on that fug of venoms.

No wonder he raves,
no wonder he opens the window
on all that's lost. What he mourns, forever
weaves into vacancy. Every grappling muscle
loosens a little, though, when the air slides in –
soft, cool, benevolent:
any breeze off any ocean.

Task

Edmond Jabès

When you have dropped the book
and that book commences
plummeting
and earth's rent
by its pure descent;

stone crackles and splits
beneath it, and the book
goes on through bedrock,
through the spluttering molten enclaves;

released, given-up,
neither use nor ornament, then
you must take up your pen
(so heavy now – the pen
is heavy as time, as fate);

you must lift up your pen
as if it weighed nothing.

Acknowledgements

The following poems have appeared in *Poetry Wales* magazine: The Titans, Sermon, Anthropology, The Damage, Country Boy, The Space of Saying, Pilgrim, The Banner, The Just, Emanations, Tincture, Domestic, Druid's Altar, Le Maudit Maudit, White-Out. The last ten of these also appeared in *The Pterodactyl's Wing* (Parthian, 2003). White-Out also appeared in *Poetry Wales – Forty Years* (Seren, 2005).

Quitting the Premises, From the Battlements, and Radioactive appeared in the online magazine *Big Bridge* (no. 11).